# GETTING STARTED IN
# OILS

Brian and Ursula Bagnall • Astrid Hille

WALTER FOSTER PUBLISHING, INC.
Tustin, California

Published by Walter Foster Publishing, Inc.,
430 West Sixth Street, Tustin, CA 92680-9990.
All rights reserved.
English translation copyright © 1994 Joshua Morris
Publishing, Inc., 221 Danbury Road, Wilton, CT 06897.
Produced by Joshua Morris Publishing, Inc.
© 1993 by Ravensburger Buchverlag Otto Maier GmbH.
Original German title: *Ölmalerei einfach anfangen.*
Cover painting by Brian Bagnall.
Printed in Hong Kong.

ISBN: 1-56010-178-4
10 9 8 7 6 5 4 3 2 1

# Contents

# About This Book

Many people feel that oil painting is the only kind of painting that deserves to be called art. This awe of oil painting seems to make the average person think, "I could never do anything like that!" This attitude has a lot to do with the fact that the most famous artists painted in oils. Famous oil paintings hang in prominent museums, and in art history classes students are confronted with the old masters of oil painting. Even among such modern painters as the surrealists, oil painting seems to be a skill that is difficult to learn—something almost unattainable.

You can overcome the fear of oil painting with the help of the artists who share their knowledge and experience in these pages. Oil is a patient medium. It can be worked and reworked, and it can withstand lengthy pauses—but it is also a medium that requires patience. Because quick, effective results are difficult to achieve with oils, you have to plan a painting and think about it carefully. However, you can use some tricks that make it easier to create the image you want, and it is almost always possible to fix an oil painting.

This book will help you to learn and apply the techniques of oil painting and to develop your own style. Different artists provide step-by-step examples of their personal approach to oil painting. They experiment with the medium, give you practical tips, and suggest ways in which you can continue to develop your skills on your own. The main concern, however, is to help you learn how much fun it can be to paint in oils.

As a teacher of painting used to say, "You have to want to bite into the paints—the enjoyment of a good meal is nothing compared to the enjoyment of oil painting." So let's dig in!

## Ursula Bagnall

Ursula Bagnall is the partner of Brian Bagnall, the art director of the Artist's Workshop series, and she is responsible for the text and layout. She brings together the artists' diverse outlooks, explanations, and paintings between the two covers of this book.

Ursula Bagnall was born in 1945 and completed her training in graphic design at the Akademie für Graphisches Gewerbe, in Munich. Afterward, she worked with Otl Aicher on projects for the 1972 Olympic Games and later took a five-year teaching position at an American school in Amsterdam. In addition to completing free-lance assignments for the Bavarian television station, she has worked since 1973 as a free-lance graphic artist and author. She has coauthored many books with Brian Bagnall, among them several art instruction books for children and adults.

## Astrid Hille

Astrid Hille is the editor of the Artist's Workshop series and works closely with Bagnall Studios. She was born in 1955 in Hamburg, Germany, where she completed training as a technical illustrator at the Fachhochschule für Kunst und Gestaltung. She went on to further study of illustration and painting and then worked as an illustrator and painter as well as an art teacher in adult education programs. A resident of Freiburg, Germany, since 1982, Hille has completed a second degree in multimedia education and has been a proofreader of art books and children's books since 1985.

## Brian Bagnall

Brian Bagnall shows how to paint a simple landscape in oils. Born in 1943 in Wakefield, England, Brian Bagnall studied painting and printmaking and completed his National Diploma with honors. He then moved to Amsterdam, where, in addition to teaching, he worked for numerous publishing houses and advertising agencies. He was also active for many years as a professor in Darmstadt, Germany.

Since 1970, Brian Bagnall has lived in Munich, where he and his wife, Ursula, opened Bagnall Studios. He has written many books, and his work has been exhibited all over Europe and Korea.

## Edeltraut Klapproth

Edeltraut Klapproth shows readers step-by-step that it isn't at all difficult to create oil paintings of colorful flowers. She grew up in the city of Dachau, Germany, home to many painters. While she was in Munich in the 1920s, she took lessons from a number of well-known painters. Her artistic endeavors were interrupted by marriage and World War II, and she was not able to begin them again until her children were grown. Klapproth enjoyed surprising success at her first exhibit. Without regard for contemporary trends, she displays her work at least twice a year.

## Florentine Kotter

Florentine Kotter demonstrates her unique style by showing how to paint a still life. Born in 1955 in Munich, she studied art there at the Akademie der bildenden Künste, where she also took master classes. Since earning her degree, she has been a successful free-lance artist and a teacher of both private and high-school students. She has been an instructor at the painting academy of the Münchner Bildungswerk, in Munich, since 1991. Kotter did the painting below, *Sitting Woman*, in 1989.

## Uwe Neuhaus

Uwe Neuhaus shares his dreams and guides you step-by-step to a fantasy island he has painted. Neuhaus was born in 1942 in Mittenwald, Germany, and studied graphic design and painting in Munich. In 1966, he opened the smallest gallery in Munich and enjoyed much success with his outlandish and unconventional paintings. He has taken part in numerous solo and group exhibitions in Germany, Italy, and Switzerland. The son of an actor, Neuhaus holds annual exhibits in his farmhouse in the Allgäu area of Germany. These exhibits, which combine satire and cabaret, are so popular that he has appeared in two television documentaries.

# Oil Painting–Yesterday and Today

Almost all the famous paintings people know from art history classes and museums are oil paintings. It is no surprise, then, that most observers assume that oil is one of the oldest painting media. Yet oil painting is relatively young: the ancient Egyptians, for example, mixed their pigments with water. In spite of its youth, however, oil painting long held the rank of the only "true" pictorial art. Very few artists of the fifteenth and sixteenth centuries would have thought of a watercolor painting as a work of art.

The first examples of oil painting date to the twelfth century, appearing in a textbook by the artist-monk Theophilus. A lot of experimenting had to be done, however, before artists could use pure oil paints as a medium. At first, artists worked with oil-based tempera paints made from resins.

Art history books often cite Jan van Eyck (1390-1441) as the originator of modern oil painting. This famous painter, who was a founder of the so-called Flemish School, began to bind his earth pigments with linseed oil and a kind of turpentine. This breakthrough created many new possibilities for painters. Van Eyck found that he could control the drying time of his paints, thereby increasing the amount of time he could spend working

Jan van Eyck, *Madonna with Chancellor Rolin*

Rembrandt, *Saskia and Rembrandt*

on a painting. Yet Van Eyck's pictures involved more than simply applying oil paints; like his predecessors' work, they depended on special mixing techniques. Van Eyck was also the first artist to employ a special layering technique in his paintings. He applied the base with a thin resin oil and painted over it with fat-oil temperas.

Van Eyck's innovations had an enduring influence on oil painting. His ideas spread to Florence, Italy, where Leonardo da Vinci (1452-1519) studied them and continued experimenting with oils, lacquers, and resins. In Venice, the young Titian (1488/90-1576)—who would become the most influential painter of the sixteenth century—familiarized himself with the style of Van Eyck. He continued to develop Van Eyck's techniques and revolutionized painting to such an extent that art historians speak of an epoch "before Titian" and an epoch "after Titian." Titian went beyond the thin oil glazes Van Eyck had mastered;

production of oil paints begin, and around 1850 the first oil paints in zinc tubes appeared on the market. This standardized palette was critical in opening new expressive possibilities to the Impressionists, who were concerned with the interplay of light and color.

Artists in the twentieth century continued to explore the potential of oil painting. The Impressionists influenced the young Picasso (1881-1973) during his many trips to Paris, but Picasso took his fascination with color in an entirely different direction. He painted for a few years exclusively in blue hues; art historians call these years from 1901 to 1904 the Blue Period. Later, Picasso's palette broadened, but pink hues predominated (the so-called Rose Period of 1904-1906). Inspired by Cézanne, Picasso next concentrated on the geometric structures in a painting.

**Vincent van Gogh,**
***The Bridge at Arles***

he painted with thick, opaque colors and was not concerned with small details in his paintings.

Pure oil painting finally established itself in the seventeenth century. Peter Paul Rubens (1577-1640) and Rembrandt (1606-1669), the master of contrast, are among the best-known artists of this period. Again and again, Rembrandt's rather dark paintings contain the same texture, the same interplay of light and shadow. Only the main elements of his paintings are lighted—sometimes flooded with light—but the light source is difficult to define. The rest of the scene remains in shadows and darkness.

Rembrandt did not subscribe to any rules of technique. He worked with thick paints, similar in consistency to the oil paints of today, and applied thick layers of color. Yet he also mastered the technique of applying color thinly, and his paintings often contain thin glazes over thick, generous layers of paint. Rembrandt frequently scratched his paintings with the end of his brush to create textures—a practice quite unconventional for his time.

The years shortly before and after Rembrandt created his masterpieces saw important developments in the materials oil painters use. For example, the canvas that today is part of the painter's standard equipment was introduced relatively late. At first, a wooden panel soaked with glue served as the painting surface. In the 1500s, however, at the end of the Renaissance

**Pablo Picasso,** ***Fruit Bowl and Guitar***

and the beginning of Mannerism, very large paintings became popular, and the wooden panels became too small. At this time, artists began painting on canvas and using easels.

The technical improvements made during the seventeenth century in the production of oil paints were also important for modern painting. In previous centuries, artists had to produce their own oil paints, and it was not easy to create the same colors consistently. Not until the final third of the eighteenth century did mass

Finally, he began to experiment with shapes and thus paved the way for cubism. In his later works, dissolving shapes resulted in complete abstraction.

From the twelfth-century textbook of Theophilus, through the rich textures of Rembrandt and the abstract designs of Picasso and the cubists, to the work of late-twentieth-century artists and those who will follow them, it has been a long road to the oil painting the world knows today.

# Choosing Materials

If you are completely new to oil painting, you may be shocked at all the materials you need. At first, you should try to get by with as few items as possible and buy only the highest-quality supplies you can afford. Then, when you have developed your knowledge and skill to the point where you know what you need most, you can expand your equipment.

In the beginning, you need a limited number of colors, a small assortment of brushes, and a palette knife, which is used for mixing, scraping, and applying paints. You also need turpentine to wash out your brushes and painting medium to thin the paints. Mixing paints requires a palette: a piece of wood, paper, or plastic will do, and some artists even use a flat piece of glass. A few rags or tissues make it easy to clean your brushes.

Packaged sets of materials are practical, but they can be more expensive than

materials you individually choose yourself. Packages usually contain brushes, turpentine, painting medium, a palette, paint containers, and paints. If you buy such a set, make sure that you carefully check the colors it contains, because not all colors go together well. (Pages 12 and 13 of this book provide detailed explanations of the way oil paints mix.)

If you choose your materials yourself, three or four brushes and six to ten colors (again, see pages 12 and 13) will be enough. The most practical brushes for manipulating large amounts of oil paint are bristle brushes because they are stiff; bristle brushes are also durable, and the hairs don't stick together. Sable brushes are more suitable for fine detail work.

Both kinds of brushes—bristle and sable—are available in long and short, round and flat varieties. Longer bristles make softer brush strokes, while shorter bristles are more precise. At first, it is enough to have a long round brush, a standard flat brush, and a fine, short-bristled flat brush. While you're working, you can use a holder to keep the tips of your brushes suspended in a container of turpentine to prevent them from being damaged (see below, in front of the easel).

Turpentine and painting medium are available in small bottles. Turpentine is used to wash the brushes, painting medium to thin the paints. Different painting mediums—usually a mixture of soft-resin varnish, wax, and linseed oil—dry at different rates, depending on the amount of medium you mix with the paint. The slow-drying mediums are best for thinning paints, and you can paint on the fast-drying ones in a few hours; in between are the mediums that require several days to dry. You can store painting medium in virtually any container, the most practical one being a small cup that can be attached to the palette.

You can work anyplace where there is room for your materials. It's your choice whether to lay the canvas on a table or to use an easel. Easels are available in all sizes: small, which can be placed on a table, and large, which stand on the floor or ground. You can also buy an easy-to-carry folding easel. In any case, don't be afraid to set up easels in the store to see which type you're most comfortable with—after all, you're the one who has to work with it.

Finally, an oil painter is well-advised to wear a smock or an apron while working. It is very easy to get paint on your clothing, and oil paints are difficult to remove.

# Preparation and Getting Started

Aside from the selection of a motif, the actual preparation for oil painting begins with the work space. To work undisturbed—and to avoid having to interrupt your painting to get something you need—you should organize your work space so that all your materials and equipment are easily accessible. You should also have a comfortable seat and a good light source.

## The Painting Surface

You can paint on almost any kind of surface, as long as you prime it properly. You can use thick paper, cardboard, canvas, or wood. For the beginner, it is simplest to use preprimed, prestretched canvas or preprimed blocks of paper. You can then paint over this white surface with a color to establish the basic mood of the painting. Edeltraut Klapproth shows you how to do this in her step-by-step description that begins on page 38.

**Primed and unprimed linen**

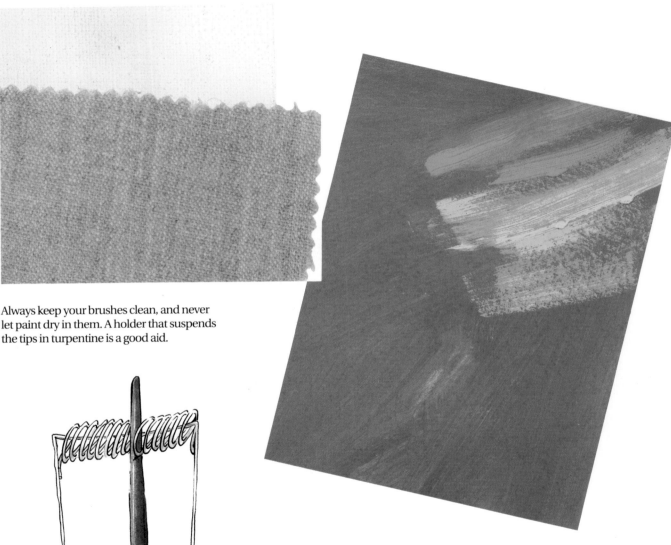

Always keep your brushes clean, and never let paint dry in them. A holder that suspends the tips in turpentine is a good aid.

A ready-to-use white primer, called gesso, is applied to untreated canvas. You can thin gesso with water and apply as little or as much as you need. In general, paint over gesso appears soft, and the colors are easy to blend.

If you want to paint on cardboard or a similar surface, you have to be careful that the oil doesn't soak into the surface and form ugly blotches. Above, for example, a painter has used fast-drying painting medium on a piece of gray cardboard.

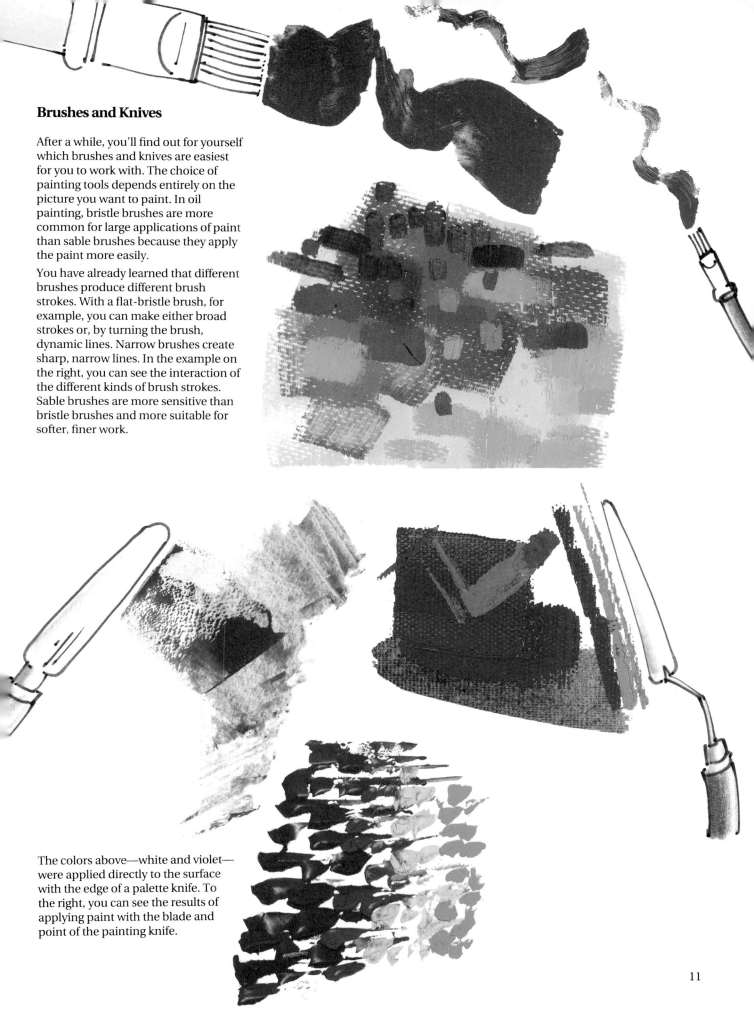

## Brushes and Knives

After a while, you'll find out for yourself which brushes and knives are easiest for you to work with. The choice of painting tools depends entirely on the picture you want to paint. In oil painting, bristle brushes are more common for large applications of paint than sable brushes because they apply the paint more easily.

You have already learned that different brushes produce different brush strokes. With a flat-bristle brush, for example, you can make either broad strokes or, by turning the brush, dynamic lines. Narrow brushes create sharp, narrow lines. In the example on the right, you can see the interaction of the different kinds of brush strokes. Sable brushes are more sensitive than bristle brushes and more suitable for softer, finer work.

The colors above—white and violet— were applied directly to the surface with the edge of a palette knife. To the right, you can see the results of applying paint with the blade and point of the painting knife.

# Mixing Oil Paints

Mixing colors is the best way to familiarize yourself with the properties and qualities of oil paints. You'll need a palette that is not too small and a basic selection of nine or ten colors. Of course, you can buy many more colors, but it is important to work with colors that go together well. Some colors can result in muddy hues when mixed.

You should have a warm (cadmium) and a cool (alizarin) red, a warm (ultramarine) and a cool (cerulean) blue,

a warm (cadmium) and a cool (lemon) yellow, chromium oxide green, yellow ochre, ivory black (a deep black with no brown), and titanium white.

White is an important color in oil painting, so buy a large tube. For general use, titanium white is better than flake white or zinc white because it covers better. Moreover, flake white is highly poisonous; do not allow it to come into contact with sores or sensitive areas of the skin.

Arrange the colors on the outer edge of the palette so you can mix in the center, and leave enough space between the colors to prevent unintentional mixing while you paint.

**titanium white**

**cadmium yellow**

**yellow ochre**

**cadmium red**

**alizarin crimson**

**chromium oxide green**

**ivory black**

**ultramarine blue**

**cerulean blue**

**(Note: The projects in this book call for a much greater variety of colors.)**

Don't mix more than three colors together at first; with more than three, it's easy to produce muddy hues. The two examples at the right show the results of mixing primary colors. In general, the hues mixed with white are cooler, those mixed with black warmer.

Paints are mixed differently depending on the technique to be used. Some artists mix directly on the canvas to achieve a multicolored texture; others mix delicate hues on the palette specifically to avoid texture.

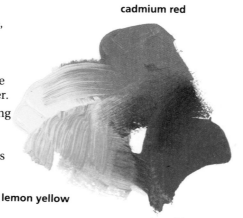

**cadmium red**

**titanium white**

**lemon yellow**

**cerulean blue**

**ultramarine blue**

**cadmium red**

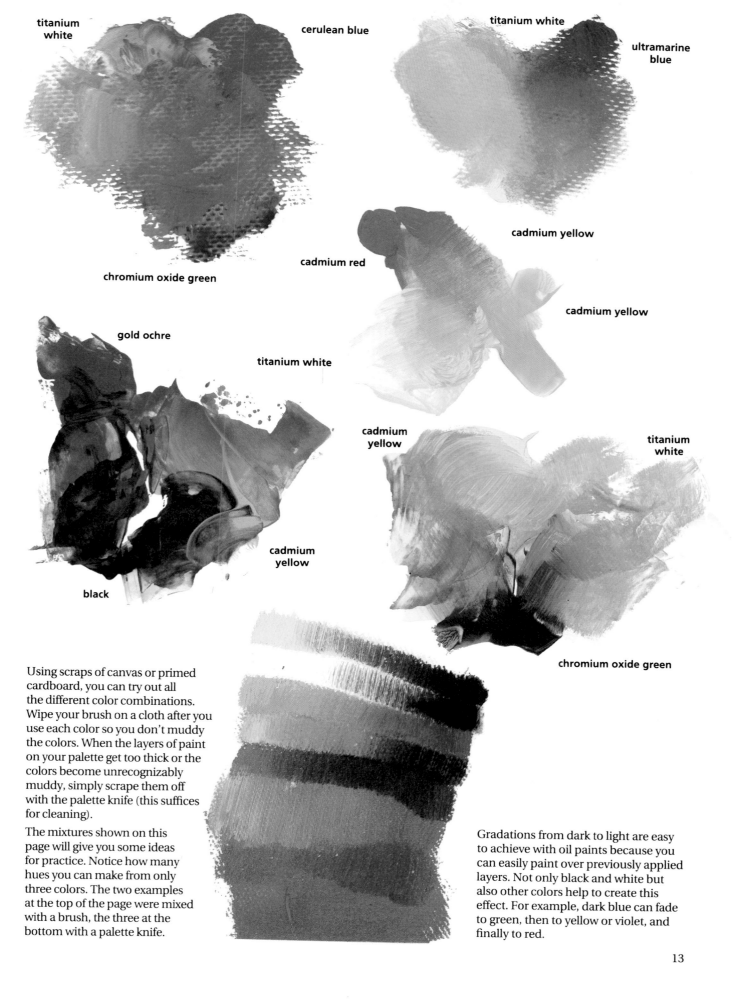

titanium white

cerulean blue

titanium white

ultramarine blue

cadmium yellow

cadmium red

cadmium yellow

chromium oxide green

gold ochre

titanium white

cadmium yellow

cadmium yellow

titanium white

black

chromium oxide green

Using scraps of canvas or primed cardboard, you can try out all the different color combinations. Wipe your brush on a cloth after you use each color so you don't muddy the colors. When the layers of paint on your palette get too thick or the colors become unrecognizably muddy, simply scrape them off with the palette knife (this suffices for cleaning).

The mixtures shown on this page will give you some ideas for practice. Notice how many hues you can make from only three colors. The two examples at the top of the page were mixed with a brush, the three at the bottom with a palette knife.

Gradations from dark to light are easy to achieve with oil paints because you can easily paint over previously applied layers. Not only black and white but also other colors help to create this effect. For example, dark blue can fade to green, then to yellow or violet, and finally to red.

13

# Basic Techniques

You can apply oil paints in many different ways. You'll soon discover a way that works best for you. Generally, it is easier to use brushes for detail work than it is to use the palette knife or the painting knife. The paints mix better with brushes and can be applied more precisely.

Use painting medium, turpentine, or linseed oil to thin the paints. Paints thinned with painting medium dry fastest, while pure oil paints take longest to dry (depending on the amount of paint, they take from three weeks to three months to dry—and sometimes even longer).

## Painting Gradations

You can paint gradations from dark to light, with or without texture. In this example, the artist has applied the paint with a soft brush from top to bottom and from left to right to achieve the delicate transition from blue to white.

## Applying Glazes

A glaze is a transparent layer of paint that is applied over a base coat, allowing the color underneath to shimmer through. The glaze must be thinned, and—if you don't want the colors to mix—the underlying color should be dry. You can see this technique in the meadow and the field in the painting below.

## Working Wet-in-Wet

As its name implies, this technique involves laying wet paint into wet paint. In contrast to watercolors, however, oil paints do not run into one another. At most they blend, which can lead to some exciting effects—for example, the sky in this painting.

## Using Impasto

The impasto technique involves applying thick layers of paint that result in a raised texture you can feel with your hand. You can achieve this texture with a stiff brush or a palette knife. The key is to paint quickly, with short movements that leave the paint sticking up from the surface. Remember: if the paint contains too much oil, it won't "stand up" from the canvas very well. To avoid this problem, first squeeze the paint onto a paper towel so the excess oil is absorbed, and then use the stiffer paint that results (see the treetop in the painting below).

## Working Dry-on-Dry

The dry-on-dry technique involves applying unthinned paint to a dry background (see the yellow tree below). If you use your brush to pick up a small amount of paint and then apply it to the unpainted canvas, you can create some interesting textures (see the thin green tree on the left side of the painting).

## Using the Palette Knife and the Painting Knife

You can achieve certain textures only with a palette knife or a painting knife. This spectrum of textures ranges from broad, sweeping strokes made with the edge of the knife (left and below) to finely textured strokes made with the tip (below, in the meadow).

15

# What Colors Tell Us

**Compare the warm hues in the painting above with the cool hues in the painting below. The mood of a painting is just as important as the motif.**

There is more to painting than technique. Your paintings must be able to express moods, communicate ideas, and awaken feelings in the viewer. It is therefore important to know the effects that colors have and what you can express with them. As a start, consider two basic categories of color: warm and cool. The concepts of warm and cool arise from the associations these colors suggest. Blue gives the impression of coolness; it reminds viewers of deep, cold water, snow, and ice. Red and yellow hues give a feeling of warmth; after all, these are the colors of fire and the sun.

Hues are not always this easy to categorize. Some colors lie in the midrange between warm and cool and have a more neutral effect—for example, red-violet and yellow-green. It is possible, therefore, to have a cool red and a warm blue if the red contains a lot of blue or the blue contains a lot of red. As a general rule, you can make a color warmer by adding yellow and cooler by adding blue.

There are no rules that state when to use which colors; you have to decide this for yourself. To be able to make a decision, however, you have to be familiar with the effects of colors. Compare the two examples at the left. Both contain the same motif, but the colors are different. The painting at the top captures the feeling of a warm summer day, while the one at the bottom has a cool, overcast effect.

Try making a few small, simple sketches of a single motif (an abstract motif will work for the purposes of this experiment), using color to express warmth or coolness. Bear in mind that cadmium red gives you warm hues, and alizarin crimson produces cool hues.

When colors "flicker" (see the example above), the image can be striking but also disturbing. This effect occurs when colors with the same intensity are placed next to each other, and it is especially noticeable in combinations of red and green, red and blue, and orange and green. Pop artists, such as Roy Lichtenstein and Andy Warhol, intentionally used this effect to make their paintings livelier. Avoid it, however, if you want to paint a tranquil motif.

Naturally, colors can express more than warmth or coolness. A painting's color scheme alone can express happiness or sadness, peacefulness or aggressiveness. A painting of a crying child with a pale face looks much sadder than one of a crying child with rosy cheeks. The color of live or freshly picked plants is entirely different from the color of dead or wilted ones. Using pastels or colored pencils, you can create a few simple sketches to experiment with the emotional aspects of color. The two examples at the right will give you some ideas. The picture at the top is bright and happy, while the one at the bottom is sad and melancholy. Try to depict spring and fall using only color—no motif.

# Simplifying Your Motif and Putting It on Paper

To transfer what you see onto paper, you have to be able to simplify. It is impossible, for example, to paint all the leaves on a tree. You have to try to capture the shape and feeling of the tree instead. Basic shapes, such as the circle, the square, and the triangle, can be a big help in this effort. When you look around your home, you can find many things that have one of these three shapes as their basis—for example, a round teapot or a square table.

In the photo above, a view of an Italian village with a tower, the shapes seem very complicated; yet they are actually only squares and triangles, as you can see in the sketch at the left. Reducing objects to their basic shapes is always a good exercise to simplify complex motifs. Make a few simple sketches of familiar objects. Try not to get lost in details; instead, concentrate on the most important shapes. The pattern on a vase is not important, for example, but the shape of the vase is. In the example sketch here, the trees and bushes serve mainly as decoration.

A painting should be more than a mere copy of nature. You can leave out unimportant or disturbing elements, such as power lines, and you can add such elements as trees or flowers. In this example, the artist simplified the trees and bushes in the foreground, using diagonal lines to make them more exciting. In the photo, the main areas—the sky, the village, the hill—are all equal; in the drawings, they have been changed a little to make the picture more interesting.

A composition is not only a matter of the positive space—that is, the motif itself—but also a matter of the negative space that surrounds the motif. The paper or canvas forms a frame around the motif. The negative space, which is just as important as the positive space, lies between the edges of this "frame" and the edges of the motif.

The negative space gives an object its form—it can either constrict the form or give it room. The picture above is reduced to positive and negative space, and you can see their distribution very clearly. You can focus on the shapes of the trees and the buildings or on the shapes of the space surrounding them.

Find a picture or photograph and trace around the negative space. The result will probably look something like the example at the right, and you'll be able to see how strongly the positive and negative spaces influence one another.

Don't be afraid to exaggerate. If you do not have the opportunity to observe your motif from different angles, try to imagine how it might look from various perspectives. Here the artist has moved the village into the background, giving the picture more depth. How would the picture look if the village were large and dominating? Experiment for yourself in a few simple sketches.

# Important Aspects of Composition

Everyone possesses a natural talent for composition. When you decorate a table, hang paintings on a wall, or arrange the living room, you are unconsciously creating a composition of objects by arranging shapes and colors. What you need to learn, then, is the conscious handling of shapes and colors. Moreover, because a painting isn't three-dimensional, you also have to create the illusion of height, depth, and distance.

In addition to linear perspective, there is aerial perspective—a purely optical perspective that cannot be measured or calculated. Distance exists between the observer and an object; the further away the observer is from the object, the more atmosphere there is between them. As a result, objects that are nearer to the observer appear darker than objects that are further away. For example, you may have seen a mountain range in which some mountains are closer than others. You'll notice that the nearer mountains are darker and the more distant ones are lighter.

This example shows five tonal variations. Without any change in the sizes of the objects, the transition from dark to light is sufficient to give the impression that the tree and the dark area are significantly closer than the lighter area in the upper portion of the painting.

To show this effect clearly, the artist has used only one color in the example. Of course, you can create the same impression using different colors.

When you look up—for example, at a church's tall steeple—atmosphere is between you and the top of the steeple. This atmosphere makes the steeple appear taller and more distant. If you want to depict something as being especially high above the ground, try painting the object so that it becomes lighter toward the top.

Remember that art has no steadfast rules. The suggestions here should merely serve as a guide to help you become a better painter. When you learn all the basic principles and know how to apply them, you can begin to throw a few of them overboard.

In addition to color and shape, the size and arrangement of objects give expression to a painting. A symmetrical, balanced composition gives the impression of tranquility. In the example above, the shapes are not exaggerated or unbalanced; the house and the tree are simply standing in the meadow.

The large house here dominates the picture—everything else recedes into the background. The impression of closeness is reinforced by the picture's top edge, which cuts off the roof of the house. When something is very close, little room remains for other elements. Here the impression of depth has been avoided to emphasize the dominance of the house.

Now the house is off in the distance. This impression is conveyed by the large area of meadow in the foreground and the extremely small shapes of the house and the tree. However, the house and the tree continue to be the focal point of the composition because of the color arrangement, that is, the green area leads the eye directly to them.

Now the tree dominates, its diagonal shape creating tension in the composition. Diagonal shapes, crooked lines, and angles have a more dynamic, aggressive effect than do round, even shapes. You can use this simple motif to sketch a few compositions. Feel free to make dramatic changes.

# Working with Light and Shadow

So far you have concentrated on simplifying shapes, working with positive and negative space, and using the expressive element of color, but you haven't yet considered the actual objects you might want to paint. If you want to paint from nature—which, by the way, is an excellent exercise for abstract painters—light and shadow will have an important influence on your picture. Light can alter colors, reflect on unwanted areas, and even change the shape of an object.

Without light and shadow, an object appears flat. Shadows indicate whether an object is resting on a surface or floating in space. Take a look at a simple shape—a cube. From the front, a cube is a flat square. Even a perspective drawing is ambiguous until the artist adds the shadows. The shadow on an object itself is called the core shadow.

The shadow that an object throws indicates its position relative to the light source. This is called the cast shadow, and it changes visibly in different lighting conditions.

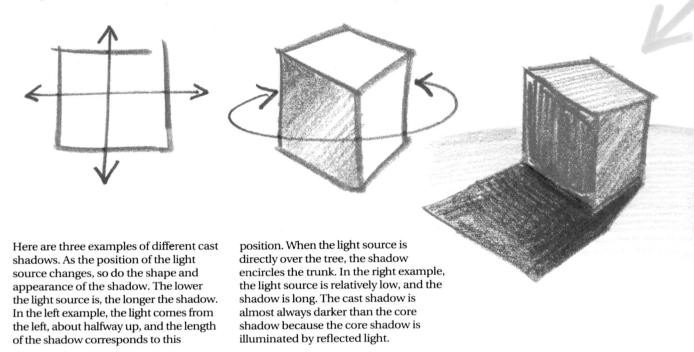

Here are three examples of different cast shadows. As the position of the light source changes, so do the shape and appearance of the shadow. The lower the light source is, the longer the shadow. In the left example, the light comes from the left, about halfway up, and the length of the shadow corresponds to this position. When the light source is directly over the tree, the shadow encircles the trunk. In the right example, the light source is relatively low, and the shadow is long. The cast shadow is almost always darker than the core shadow because the core shadow is illuminated by reflected light.

Colors also change in shadow, losing brightness and certain nuances. The value and color of a shadow are influenced not only by light but also by surrounding objects. You can see this effect in the simple example above. Do the shadows in all three pictures have the same tonal value, or are some darker or lighter?

In fact, all of them have the same tonal value, yet if the background is very light, the shadow seems darker. The darker the background, however, the lighter the shadow appears.

Train your observational skills: Take a simple object—a box or a vase—and expose it to several different light sources, or shine a light on it from

different angles. Carefully observe the shadows, the way the shadows change, and the color of the surroundings. Sketch the differences with pastels or colored pencils. This exercise is especially helpful if you want to paint still lifes, but it is useful for painting any object.

Shadows are not gray or black. They reflect the colors of their surroundings, especially the surface they are cast on. If several objects are in a group, they cast one shadow, which can assume an almost abstract shape. Unfortunately, there is no formula to help painters figure out how much of a particular color a shadow contains. You have to rely on your own judgment for that. Because the surface in this example is pink and the sphere is blue, the artist chose a violet hue, in which the colors of the cube and the pyramid are reflected.

You can see clearly that the light comes from the upper right. The violet of the cast shadow can also be found in the core shadow. The highlights are important, too, and they should be added last.

# Creating a Painting

A finished painting provides a focus for discussion of what you've learned so far. You should always begin your picture by making a few preliminary sketches, because they will help you become acquainted with the distribution of shapes and the important and unimportant parts of the motif. Some painters use oil pastels to do this because they most closely simulate oil paints. In the sketches here, you can already see the interplay of shapes: the flowers are the focal point of the painting, but they do not overwhelm it. The sketch also includes the light and dark values. Of course, making more than one sketch allows you try out several different compositions.

Positive and negative space also plays an important role in the composition, as you can see in the sketch at the right. Be sure to plan even the smallest shapes because coincidental overlappings or angles and corners that suddenly appear can destroy a composition. Although the large surface areas form the main elements in the composition, they don't detract from the vase—they lead the eye toward it.

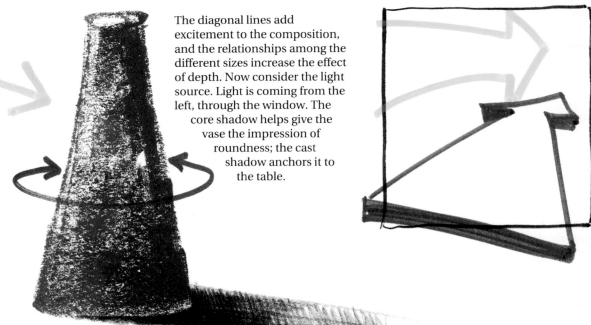

The diagonal lines add excitement to the composition, and the relationships among the different sizes increase the effect of depth. Now consider the light source. Light is coming from the left, through the window. The core shadow helps give the vase the impression of roundness; the cast shadow anchors it to the table.

Look more closely at the cast shadow. It isn't simply brown—rather, it reflects the reds and violets that are found in the flowers and the vase. Similarly, the walls are not simply painted one flat color. They get their colors from the hues in the other elements of the painting, such as the orange that is repeated throughout.

This color scheme ties the painting together. In general, you should avoid painting areas in just one color. Look at an exterior wall, for example: you can find shadows, spots or marks, or even colors reflected from trees or cars. Such colors can be an important artistic element in a painting.

To capture the wood texture of the table, the artist thinned the paint and applied it in glazes. Although you may not have noticed them at first, the highlights on the table's legs and edges are also very important.

# How Others Have Done It

**Georges Seurat,**
***Bridge at Courbevoie***

## Georges Seurat
## 1859-1891

Even as a student, the French painter Georges Seurat was a very careful observer of nature, and he was exceptionally methodical in his studies. He retained this thoroughness throughout his career. When he painted, he carefully observed the interplay of light and shadow in his motif before he made the first brush stroke on the canvas—or, perhaps more accurately, before he made the first dot on the canvas. Seurat developed a unique style called pointillism, in which he applied the paint in many small dots rather than with large strokes. In this way, he could paint a meadow of blue and yellow points, and it would appear green—a phenomenon that occurs because of the eye's ability to "mix" colors optically. The reflections of the sky in the meadow are depicted with blue dots, those of the sun with yellow or orange. This technique allows the colors to extend a mood over an entire painting.

Seurat had a distinctive way of arranging his palette (above left). The first column contained unmixed colors, the next column contained the same colors mixed with white, and the final column contained pure white. He almost always used the same colors in his paintings, but they never seem monotonous because of the different ways he arranged them.

*Bridge at Courbevoie* (18" x 21.5") is an especially well planned composition in which horizontal and vertical lines are arranged carefully. The painting is similar to a low-resolution photograph: the more you look at it, the more colors you discover. Notice the pink hues that are spread throughout the painting. They hold the painting together without dominating it.

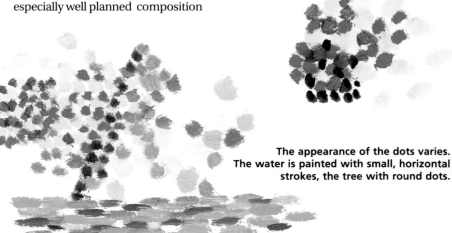

**The appearance of the dots varies. The water is painted with small, horizontal strokes, the tree with round dots.**

Flat brushes are best for making sharp lines and hard edges.

Lyonel Feininger, *Side Wheeler II*

# Lyonel Feininger
## 1871-1956

Lyonel Feininger came from a German-American family, who planned for him to study music in Berlin. He began to draw, however, and he eventually became an illustrator and caricaturist for several periodicals. As a caricaturist, he routinely distorted reality. When he was 30 years old, he decided to become a painter, and approximately 10 years later he discovered cubism.

His painting *Side Wheeler II* (32" x 39.5") shows an unusual disintegration of perspective and shape. Waves, such as the ones you see at the seashore, are usually soft and round; here they are triangular and pointed. Feininger consciously incorporates cool and warm hues as a form of perspective: the warm colors come to the foreground, and the cooler colors recede, adding depth to the painting. He uses a glazing technique, often going over the paints with a dry brush. Flat brushes are especially suitable for this type of work.

The layering of textures adds special appeal to a painting. You can achieve this effect by applying thin glazes. The warm reds and yellows come to the foreground, while the cooler hues recede into the background.

Paul Cézanne, *Still Life with Teapot*

# Paul Cézanne
## 1839-1906

Still lifes were the favorite motif of the French painter Paul Cézanne, who was fascinated by their permanence and lack of movement. Sometimes he laid coins beneath round pieces of fruit so the fruit would remain exactly where he placed it, and on occasion he even painted artificial flowers so his motif wouldn't wilt. He spent a lot of time arranging the objects in the composition, and the flow of the cloth under the objects was also very important to him. He had an especially abundant array of colors, which he always mixed on the palette—never on the canvas itself.

In the detail at the left, you can see how Cézanne used color. The pieces of fruit and the teapot are accurately modeled; the colors of the fruit are reflected in the teapot and the table.

## Vincent van Gogh
## 1853-1890

The Dutch painter Vincent van Gogh had a uniquely personal painting style. He applied many strokes of thick—often unmixed—paint on top of and next to one another, lending a lively mood to his still lifes. In contrast to Cézanne, he painted spontaneously, always drawing inspiration from light and color. He intentionally put cool and warm colors next to each other, and his visible brush strokes gave form to the objects he painted.

The direction of Van Gogh's brush strokes emphasized the shape of the object. In the example here, the brush strokes of the table lead away from the vase in straight lines that extend in two directions; on the vase itself, the brush strokes follow the contour of the shape. The flowers are painted with very thick colors that mix on the canvas. Van Gogh often squeezed paint directly from the tube onto the canvas and then worked it with a brush or knife.

**Vincent van Gogh,**
*Fritillary Plant*

The example at the left simplifies Van Gogh's technique somewhat. After the base coat is applied (it can shine through if you like), the shapes are developed with strokes and dots. The colors you use can be different from the actual colors of the object—the overall impression is the main concern. The above example demonstrates a stroke that allows the colors to mix on the canvas.

# Sketches

Even artists as famous as Leonardo da Vinci and Michelangelo made sketches in which they jotted down ideas for future paintings or captured details of a motif. These drawings, which are actually studies, have a certain charm in their spontaneity.

The role of sketching is no different today. Making sketches is more personal than taking a photograph. You can use your sketchbook to capture impressions, study faces, or discover compositions in a landscape, and you can use these ideas for future paintings if you wish. Because sketches do not have to be perfect, they're often free and uninhibited.

Sketching has a special value in oil painting, because pictures must be planned. Some artists like to make sketches with oil pastels, as oil-pastel techniques resemble those of oil painting. Other painters make several watercolor sketches before they begin a work in oil.

Sketch as much as possible, because sketching will give you confidence in creating compositions as well as in transferring your ideas to paper. Pastels allow you to make color sketches in which you capture mood and expression, and you can later transfer them to oil paintings.

Because you can paint with oils on a dark background, you might want to make sketches on colored paper. This technique produces vivid color combinations and sharp contrasts.

The village on the hill (above) began as a quick pencil sketch, to which colored accents in oil pastel were added later.

The sketch below was made with a combination of colored pencils and pastels. The artist drew the pieces of fruit from nature, then imagined the tables and added them with a felt marker.

This small landscape sketch, made in colored pencil during a vacation trip, shows the artist's fascination with the geometric lines of the telephone wires in the middle of a sparsely populated area.

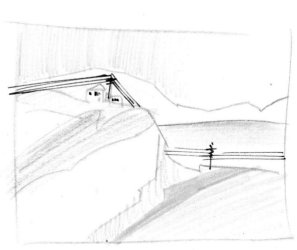

# In Greece

## with Brian Bagnall

For me, sketching is one of the most important parts of a vacation. I have traveled to Greece for many years, and I'm always fascinated by the white buildings of the Cyclades Islands. The shadows form bizarre shapes on the bright white walls of the houses; blue and red shutters and doors provide random accents.

The somewhat sparse sketches here, which have little color, depict the brightness and the heat quite well. Sometimes I discover abstract shapes between the buildings—shapes that are complemented or even intensified by plants.

Often the sketches I make lead to watercolor paintings or additional drawings. This time, however, I wanted to try to work in oils, which meant that I would have to plan the composition exactly. I had to consider such matters as the distribution of color and the interplay of shapes.

**Different views from a balcony: the large body of water between the buildings and the hills in the distance forms a unique shape.**

Using different sketches, I try to work out the most interesting composition. As you can see in the drawing above, the negative space plays just as important a role as the positive space. Four horizontal shapes are created: the sky, the hills, the water, and the row of buildings. If you change their sizes, you change the expressive element of the painting as well.

I hardly have to think about the color scheme, as the red and blue squares of the doors and windows are already where I want them. They animate the painting and draw the eye toward them.

If you like, you can sketch a few variations on the same motif. Simply try to paint areas of color, pulling them together in different sizes to form a new, perhaps abstract composition.

For my own picture, I decide to work out the sketch at the top right and transfer it to an oil painting.

33

Composition is very important to me. I often experiment with it for hours.

In this case, I trace a line drawing of my composition onto transparent paper so I can look at it from the reverse side. This strategy allows me to observe any weak areas in the design that may not be noticeable in a front view of the drawing. As soon as I am satisfied with the composition, I sketch it onto the canvas in charcoal, using as few lines as possible. If you use too much charcoal,

it can mix with the oil paints. Some painters like this type of mixing, but I don't.

With a soft, flat brush (number 4), I paint around the buildings with ultramarine blue. This color outline immediately creates distance between the buildings and the background. For the water, I apply a base coat of yellow and green because I want these colors to shimmer through later. Then I sketch in the tree with quick strokes of ochre

and umber so I can maintain control of its shape. In spite of this relatively exact planning, I have allowed myself the freedom to make changes later.

## Colors Used:

*ultramarine blue, cobalt blue, lemon yellow, chromium oxide green, yellow ochre, burnt umber, cadmium red, alizarin crimson, chrome orange, titanium white*

*I applied these colors with a number 4 and a number 12 soft, flat brush.*

The sky is reflected in the water, and the color of the sea changes with the weather. I depict this relationship between the two elements by applying a base coat of yellow to the sky. I repeat this warm hue in the foreground and in the hills, creating a harmony of color throughout the painting. The hills are not very distant, but they should nonetheless remain in the background. I set the hills apart from one another by painting them in different colors.

Next I go over the yellow sea with ultramarine blue, intentionally leaving brush-stroke textures to give the impression of movement in the water. I give the buildings, which are actually white, a base coat of yellow ochre, and then I add the colors of the windows and doors.

Now I am ready to apply the blue of the sky, remembering to allow the yellow to shimmer through. I also concentrate more on the hills: they seem darker at the point where they meet the sea; toward the top they appear lighter. Remember that objects close to the observer appear darker than those that are more distant. This is the reason why the foothills are darker than the mountaintops—they're closer. The sketch to the right shows this effect.

You may want to have another look at the discussion of aerial perspective, on pages 20 and 21.

Next I apply quick strokes of white and light blue to the water to give the impression of light shining on it. I also add warm yellows to the white buildings to bring them closer.

Polishing the details is always the last step. This is when you put in the accents and the highlights. I try to create more unity by repeating colors and adding reflections. The tree, which is actually dark, gets a little sunlight, and the red of the windows appears in the tree's leaves and in the grass. The green of the closest hill also appears in the other hills, and the yellow base coat shimmers throughout the painting. I lighten the sky so that it recedes further into the distance, but I don't change the texture of the water very much—I want to retain the liveliness.

The advantage of painting from a sketch that you do on vacation is that you get to relive the vacation many times over!

# Painting a Vase of Flowers

## with Edeltraut Klapproth

The tools I need to create a painting of flowers lie before my small easel. I've already applied a thin coat of oil paint to my preprimed canvas, because the white surface distracts me more than it inspires me. Moreover, artists rarely use pure white in a painting. This first coat of color usually determines the direction of my work because it creates a particular mood right from the start.

The large container holds turpentine, which I use to rinse the brushes while I'm working and after I've finished. I also have different brushes for different colors in my composition. I use flat sable brushes for large areas and round brushes for details. I use a slow-drying painting medium because I like to allow the colors to blend into one

another—a technique that is not possible with a fast-drying medium. When I take a break, I cover the medium; otherwise it dries. I have a rag ready in case I put too much paint on my canvas.

My choice of colors depends on what I want to paint and the mood I'm in. This means I don't always paint my motifs exactly as they appear. A painter can use this artistic freedom to work with colors that seem to produce a particular mood effectively.

I find it important to use the best-quality paints. You can make up for the added cost of such materials by using an inexpensive palette—pieces of wood, such as scraps from a carpenter, are all you need, and you can throw them away when you've finished.

I have organized my work space so that everything I need for painting is within easy reach of my right hand. The most important part of my preparation, however, is.still to come: the flowers. I have a garden, so I can afford to wait until the last minute to put together a bouquet. This way the flowers stay fresh.

**To be able to simplify later, you have to know how a flower actually looks. Preliminary sketches, then, are a necessity.**

Like painting flowers, arranging flowers is an art. The vase can't be too large or too small, and the flowers have to go together well in terms of both shape and color.

Even when I think I can paint certain flowers from memory, I always do a few studies. Through sketching, I discover new shapes created by shadows, changes in color that depend on the flower's freshness, or even structures in the plant itself that I never noticed before.

You can use almost anything to make your sketches: charcoal, colored pencils, or even markers. However, be careful if you use markers and your intention is to paint over the sketch. Many felt markers have water-soluble ink that runs when wet paint is applied. For this reason, I have done the sketches here in colored pencil.

In these sketches, you can see how the role of the vase changes. When it holds just a few flowers, the vase dominates the composition significantly more than it does when it contains the thick bouquet below. The shape of the vase should complement the shape of the flowers; it should support the bouquet's shape, but not overwhelm it. Thanks to my garden, I have the opportunity to combine many kinds of flowers—and if I don't paint them, they still look nice in my apartment.

I decide on a composition that shows only a small part of the vase. At this point in the painting process, I usually don't know much about my picture. Everything is still open—the shapes, the colors, the light and shadow.

First I sketch the shapes. I feel that charcoal smears too easily, so I use a fine brush and neutral-color oil paint. A certain amount of drawing skill is necessary here. I sketch in dark and light areas. The outlines, sketched with soft brush strokes, determine the distribution of positive and negative space. At this point, I gradually begin to imagine the colors more precisely, even if I don't make a final decision as to which ones I'll use. This is exactly what makes an oil painting so special: you can always change it. In fact, the medium inspires you to do so.

## Colors Used:

*violet, lemon yellow, cadmium yellow deep, cadmium red, cadmium orange, alizarin crimson, cobalt blue, burnt sienna, burnt umber, yellow ochre, olive green, olive green deep, Hooker's green, black, and titanium white*

Next I move to the flowers themselves. The flowers come to life by means of the shadows that form the individual petals, and the shadows alter the colors and their intensity. Look at a flower. A red rose, for example, has more hues than red alone: its color changes depending on its relationship to the light source. For this reason, I use several colors, not just one, to form the flowers. In this painting, I combine violet and alizarin crimson with different amounts of white, mixing the colors on the canvas itself as well as on the palette. This technique produces interesting textures. Yellow and olive green form the leaves and give them three-dimensionality.

It is not always a good idea to try to paint an exact reproduction of a motif. Simplify the shapes, and leave out the superfluous elements. Above all, try to capture the essence of your subject.

Sometimes you can't do anything wrong—everything works on the first try. At other times, nothing works at all. Don't become discouraged when difficulties arise. Take a break. Get away from your painting for a few days. The paints can handle it. Even if the bouquet wilts, you still have your sketches and, above all, your memory and creativity.

After the preliminary colors have been added to the flowers, the next step is to work on the painting's background. Soft base coats harmonize with the flowers and the dark leaves. Even though it seems unimportant, the background must be planned. You can't simply paint it any old way.

I use warm reds and yellows to paint a gradation from the green wall to the table that holds the vase. At first, the edge of the table that forms the horizontal line is unimportant to me (see detail at left). The cast shadow adds to the vase's three-dimensionality and makes it seem to stand solidly on the table.

Once I have refined the background and added the shadow, I make improvements, work out details, and try to harmonize the overall effect of the painting. I try to paint my impressions of the flowers, bringing light to the soft leaves to capture the feeling of a summer day. A sharp border between the wall and the table is not necessary. I let the two blend and use color and shadow to give the impression of depth. The warm hues are also repeated in the background.

Perhaps the most difficult aspect of painting is knowing when to quit. Is my picture done, or does it need something else? Nobody can answer this question for you. Even professional artists sometimes paint their pictures "to death." In general, it is better to quit too soon than too late—spontaneity is often more exciting than overworked detail.

# Painting a Fantasy Island

**with Uwe Neuhaus**

Preliminary sketches for an oil painting are very important for me. I can let my mind wander, experiment freely, change compositions, and try out different styles. Often the sketches themselves are little works of art, which I finish and frame.

You don't have to throw away used packing paper or paper bags that can be used for sketching, even if they have spots on them. You can use your imagination and incorporate these splotches into your composition. You can discover in them little figures, faces, plants, or landscapes, and you can use these elements in your painting.

I want to paint a small fantasy island, leaving myself free to decide spontaneously while I am painting whether it will be occupied or deserted—whether the landscape will be bare and lonely or full of plants.

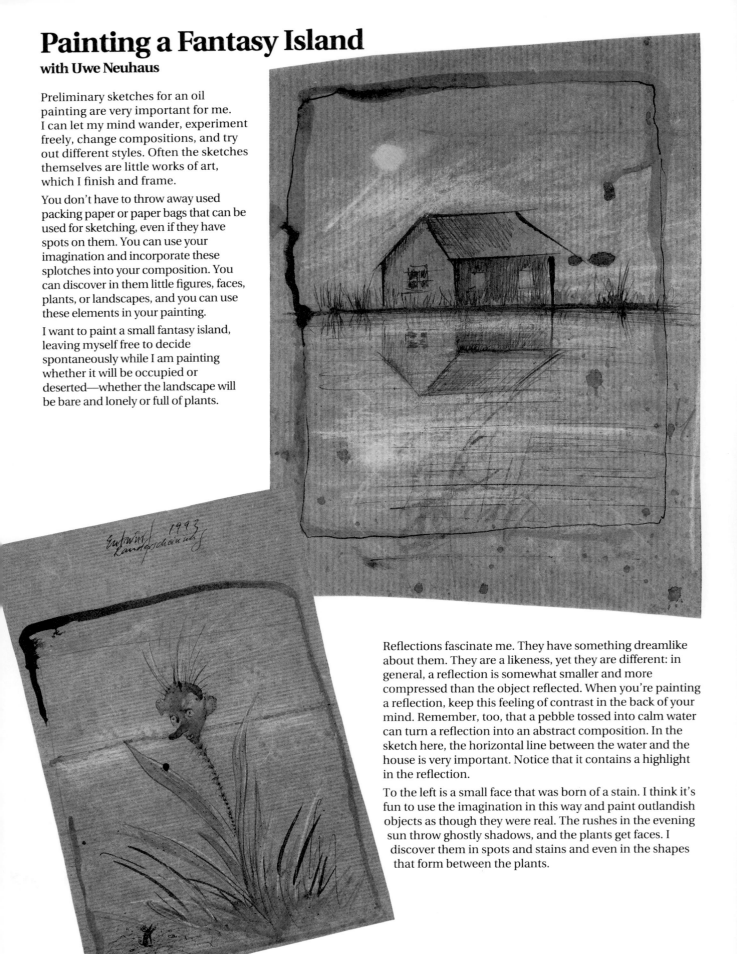

Reflections fascinate me. They have something dreamlike about them. They are a likeness, yet they are different: in general, a reflection is somewhat smaller and more compressed than the object reflected. When you're painting a reflection, keep this feeling of contrast in the back of your mind. Remember, too, that a pebble tossed into calm water can turn a reflection into an abstract composition. In the sketch here, the horizontal line between the water and the house is very important. Notice that it contains a highlight in the reflection.

To the left is a small face that was born of a stain. I think it's fun to use the imagination in this way and paint outlandish objects as though they were real. The rushes in the evening sun throw ghostly shadows, and the plants get faces. I discover them in spots and stains and even in the shapes that form between the plants.

I like to use packing paper for my sketches, and I incorporate its color and texture into them. Sometimes I even try to reproduce the paper's color and texture in my oil paintings.

As I play with the forms and the limited colors in my sketch, my island gradually begins to take shape. I use ink and a white pencil because I like the sparse colors, and I decide to use a similar color scheme in my oil painting. I choose the following colors: green earth, Prussian blue, indigo, yellow ochre, and white.

I don't always paint on canvas. Pieces of wood, Masonite, and thick cardboard can also provide excellent painting surfaces if they are primed properly. This time, I use thumbtacks to stretch tightly woven cotton across a board. Then I apply white gesso.

You can start painting as soon as the surface you're using is dry. As you've already learned, it is important to paint distant objects with light hues and closer objects with darker ones to establish a feeling of depth.

I begin with the background, that is, with the sky and water. Then I sketch in the island with a fine brush and delicate browns and add the moon and its reflection.

**The stretched canvas can be an art form in itself. Sometimes I paint small objects around the edges, build a frame around the wood, and leave the thumbtacks as part of the painting.**

46

Like a ghost, the small island begins to appear. The limited colors, applied by means of a dry-brush technique, help give the feeling of twilight. The way the landscape fades into haze and fog gives everything a feeling of unreality. Light, reflection, and shadow are very important. Remember, don't paint with pure color straight from the tube. Mix the paints, and use a lot of white.

Seas and islands in the fog have always been places for fanciful creatures. In my painting, you can see one—perhaps made of clouds—trying to catch the moon. In the reflection, the creature is being swallowed up by a gentle ripple in the water, which is painted in white and dark greens with a dry, soft brush. Incidentally, the creature had first appeared in one of my sketches—as a hair on my paper.

I use a fine brush to work out lines and contours, giving the painting more preciseness. It takes a great deal of courage to spontaneously add a line that could change the entire mood of the painting. Yet you shouldn't follow your sketch too closely. Be spontaneous and act on the inspirations that come to you while you are painting. For example, I suddenly find small, whimsical "plant goblins," which are formed by paint splashes, sitting in the rushes in the foreground of my painting.

At this point, I also work out the light and shadow more extensively. I realize that I like the island because of its sketchiness; there is something secretive in its ghostly quality.

The final step to completion is not a big one. A few details have to be worked out and corrected. I put a delicate red on the roof of the house and repeat it in the reflection. I also use the same red in the rushes, adding thickness and color without making the painting overly colorful. The horizontal line, which separates the island and the reflection, is darker on the island and lighter in the water. I emphasize the hues that are already in the painting because too many bold colors will destroy its dreaminess.

At last, I know the title — *Simply Romantic.*

# Painting a Still Life

**with Florentine Kotter**

Arranging the different elements that will appear in your picture is part of working on the painting. Take time to experiment with shapes, sizes, and materials. I feel that simple shapes are the most interesting because they leave the most room for creativity.

When I start to plan a still life, I see not only the bowl or the vase itself but also the shapes and spaces around it, whether they are shadows or intentional overlappings. Right from the start, I make sketches that incorporate these shapes into the structure of the composition—and I make a lot of sketches, some in color using tempera paints (because they are easy to mix with white) and some in black and white using charcoal. The sketches give me the opportunity to play with my motif. The actual objects serve only as a guide; I change them in my sketches.

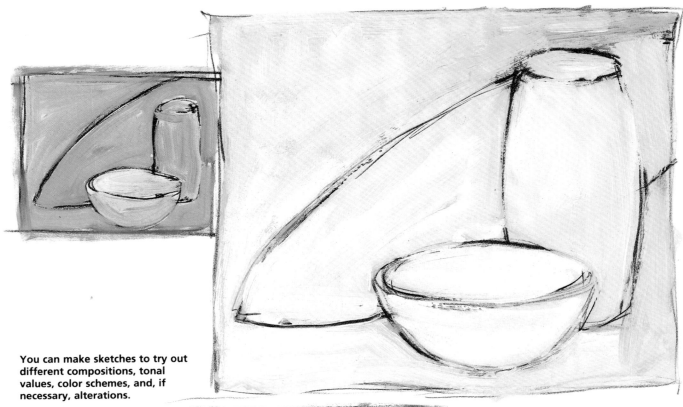

You can make sketches to try out different compositions, tonal values, color schemes, and, if necessary, alterations.

Here you can see a few examples of my sketches. I begin the color drawings with charcoal, which I partially paint over and sometimes even wipe away completely. My aim is to become completely familiar with the overall composition—with the position and balance of the shapes.

Black-and-white studies are important to establish light and shadow, which give form to the motif.

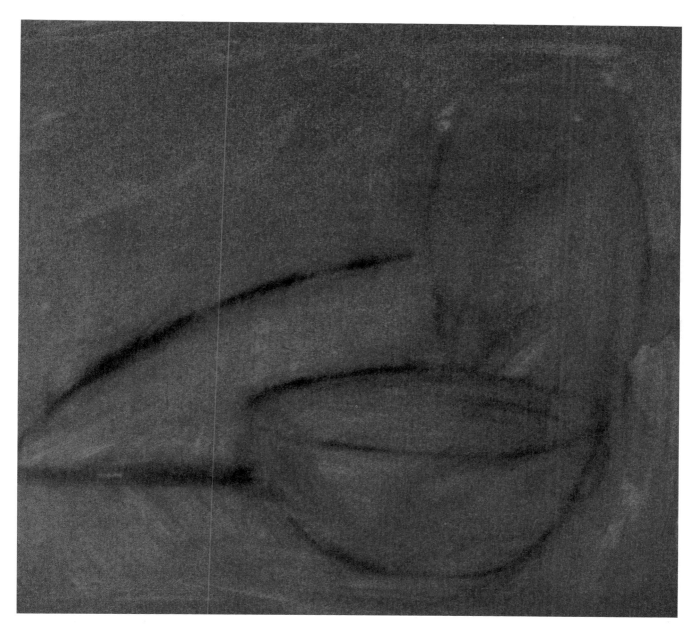

I use charcoal to make a rough sketch of the composition on the primed canvas (left). At this point, I basically sketch in the individual elements where they will be placed in the painting; I develop the details during the actual painting process.

I decide to paint the round, fat containers in earth colors, reinforcing the connection between the baked clay of the pottery and nature. The first step involves applying a base coat—a mixture of English red (light red) and cadmium yellow—over the primer. Of course, the charcoal mixes with the paint, and soon the outlines of the shapes become faint (which doesn't bother me). The white primer can also show through.

Learn to view the creation of a painting as a process of constant change, a process in which you experiment with shapes and colors. Don't let the objects or even your own expectations inhibit you. Be open to all kinds of inspiration.

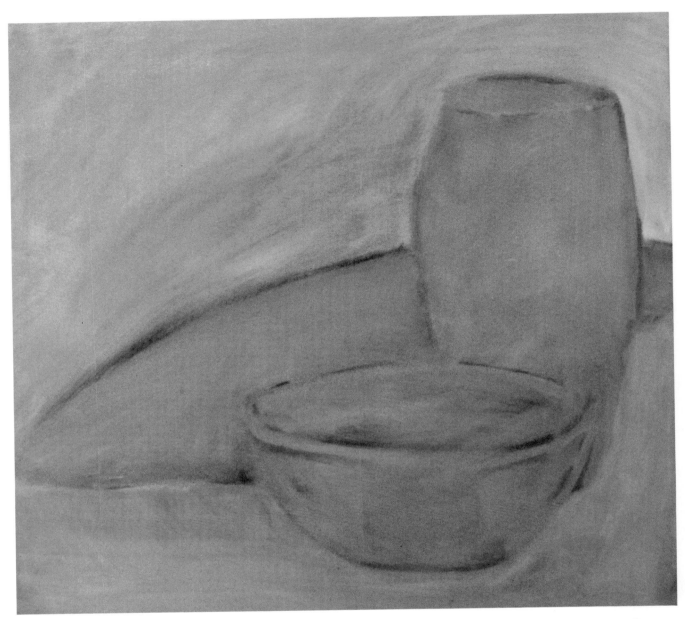

## Colors Used:

*English red (light red), cadmium yellow, brilliant yellow light, flesh ochre, burnt umber, Prussian blue, titanium white*

The foremost purpose of the dark orange-colored undercoat (clearly illustrated on page 51) is to create a base, which should only shimmer through subsequent applications of paint. I paint slowly, constantly keeping an eye on the entire painting; there will be enough time later for details. At this stage, I'm not even concerned with perspective or the exactness of the shapes. I'm only interested in the position of the shapes and the intensity of the colors. I use brilliant yellow light and flesh ochre—sometimes mixed, sometimes unmixed—and I also model the background in different colors.

Never paint a large area in one flat color; this deadens it. As proof, look closely at an area in nature. You can see that the colors vary as a result of shadows, imperfections, and surrounding objects.

As I've already mentioned, when I begin a painting I mainly concentrate on the content and the theme. In this example, I continue to work the painting with burnt umber. Already there is a certain three-dimensionality and depth. I also change the composition—I make the tall container even taller, the bowl larger. Note that the picture is not out of focus. I have merely softened the contours with a soft brush.

During the course of the painting, the colors take on a life of their own and virtually force me to change the composition. I make the tall container rounder and divide up the background. I also add delicate contours of titanium white to eliminate blurriness and use brilliant yellow and flesh ochre to create shadows and highlights. I don't always paint over colors. Sometimes I remove paint with a rag or a dry brush because I like the way the colors underneath shimmer through.

The shape in the background is a piece of wood, and it helps bring the containers into the foreground. The burnt umber is dark but warm, and the yellows and ochres shimmer through lightly, adding highlights to the wood. This clear shape emphasizes the diagonal lines, but after I look at it a while I decide that it is too hard—too dominating. I am not entirely happy with the overall direction the colors are taking. What will I do?

I use white (sometimes mixed with a little Prussian blue) to simplify the entire painting. This strategy allows me to think about other possibilities. It also gives me the opportunity to decide which side the light should come from and to consider how I can distribute the weight and shadows. It is almost like starting over completely, but it is the right move because I am inspired by the shimmering colors and the flowing shapes.

Although up to this point I have not been all that concerned about the actual objects, now I look more closely at the shadows. I set up a lamp in different positions and at various distances from the objects, and I observe how the light affects them. As you know, light and shadow can change the color as well as the shape of an object.

I decide on an obvious light source, one shining from the right. This, of course, means that the right side of the objects will be lighter than the left side. I keep the same colors that I began with, which I intensify, paint over, and sometimes wipe off. The undercoat still shimmers through and determines the mood of the painting.

Now it is time to think about color. The warm hues bring the bowl and the vase into the foreground. The shape of the shadow on the wood inspires me to add shadows in the background. The dark background—which, however, is not simply one color—also serves to bring the wood into the foreground. Finally, I complete the shapes of the objects, perfect the colors, and intensify the three-dimensionality.

Remember to stand back from your painting occasionally so that you don't get caught up in the details. Many times, these details are unimportant in the overall composition. A break is also a good idea when you're unsure about something and don't know what to do next. You can often get new ideas by taking a fresh look at your painting. Don't be afraid to try something unusual. The canvas is patient, and oil paintings can always be fixed and painted over.

# Experiments

You've learned different styles and techniques, and perhaps you've even developed some favorites. Always be open to new ideas, however, and don't be afraid to try out approaches that seem unusual at first. In this section, you'll learn a few techniques that will help you achieve some interesting effects.

In the example at the right, the artist used a painting knife to apply thick, white oil paint, then went over it with oil pastels. Raw textures formed in the spots where the paint was dry, and the pastels became mixed with white in the spots where the paint was still wet. Oil paints and pastels are a good combination because they're both soluble in turpentine.

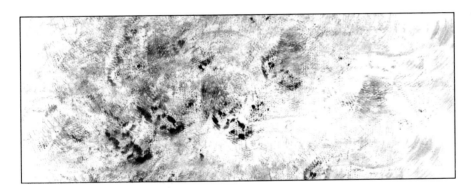

You can also scratch and scrape the wet paint as well as use a rag or sponge to apply the paint or to lift it off the canvas. You can then work with the resulting textures and incorporate them into the composition.

Below is another combination of oil paints and pastels. A relatively thin coat of paint was applied and then drawn on with different-size chalks.

The technique of frottage offers a lot of room for experimentation. The term comes from the French word *frotter,* which means "to rub." You can try the following example of this technique: lay a piece of nonabsorbent paper on wet oil paints, and press it down with your hand; when you pull the paper off, it leaves textures in the wet paint. These textures can take on very unusual shapes, and, with a little imagination, you can make some interesting paintings out of them.

In the examples above, the painter repeated this technique several times with different colors. In the example at the upper left, very thin paint was used, and it produced a completely different texture.

You can repeat frottage as much as you want, and you can do whatever you like with the resulting textures: paint on them, press on them, or scratch into them. The results will surprise you again and again. As the middle example here shows, the artist applied paint to a piece of corrugated paper and pressed it into wet paint. This results in a striped pattern. You could paint fields or meadows in this way, or even grass or other plants. How would you do it?

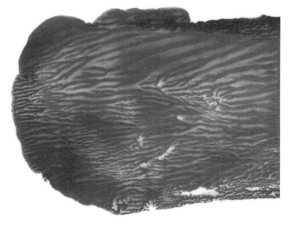

Here you can see the result of pulling off the paper. On the left is the base coat with the results of one round of frottage. On the right is the piece of tracing paper that was used.

# A Few Tips

Sometimes you feel like painting a beautiful view, so you sketch it. On paper, however, the view somehow looks boring in comparison to the real thing. In this kind of situation, it's useful to have a movable frame. To make one, simply cut two right angles out of thin cardboard or thick paper and use them to "frame" your sketches. By doing so, you can eliminate certain areas of the composition. Try framing different-size horizontal and vertical views. You'll be amazed at how exciting your sketch can be and how many variations you can find.

You can also use the movable frame with photographs that you want to paint from: certain parts of a picture are often more interesting than the entire thing. Moreover, the movable frame can save a ruined painting. Sometimes you make mistakes in only one part of a picture, while other portions of it are quite satisfying. Give the movable frame a try!

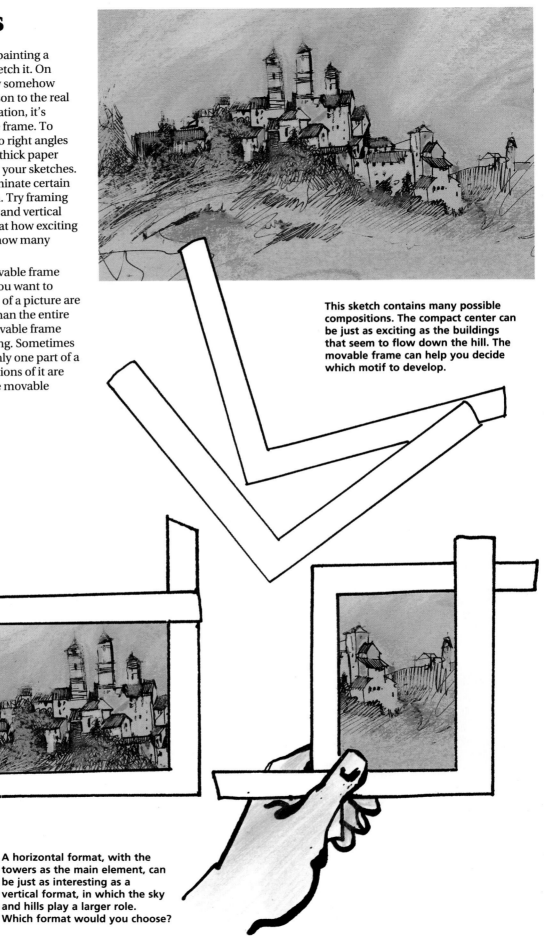

This sketch contains many possible compositions. The compact center can be just as exciting as the buildings that seem to flow down the hill. The movable frame can help you decide which motif to develop.

A horizontal format, with the towers as the main element, can be just as interesting as a vertical format, in which the sky and hills play a larger role. Which format would you choose?

## Straight Lines

Drawing straight, precise lines in oils is not everyone's cup of tea, but sometimes it's necessary. The most direct way to do this, of course, is to use a flat brush and draw the lines freehand. This technique requires a lot of practice, however, as well as a steady hand. An easier method is to support your hand on a maulstick, as in the photo below. When you do this, you have to be sure that the maulstick rests on a dry area of the painting. Another option, which is useful anytime you want a hard edge, is masking off with tape (see left).

Apply the tape to a dry surface along the edge of the area you want to create. If you want to make curves, as in the example above, cut the tape accordingly. The tape has to adhere securely so that paint can't get underneath it.

To make the line, just paint over the tape, then carefully lift the tape off when the paint is dry. If you remove the tape too quickly, you may pull away the paint. It's probably a good idea to practice this technique a few times before you try it on a painting.

## Cleaning Your Brushes

Brushes are your most important tools, so it's essential to take good care of them. When you've finished painting, clean your brushes thoroughly in brush cleaner, and then rub them in the palm of your hand. Next, wipe them on a rag, and clean them once more in soap and lukewarm water. Finally, rinse them in water, and let them dry in a container with the tips up.

# Motifs for Inspiration

Perhaps you know the feeling: you want to paint something, but you can't think of a motif. This section offers a few suggestions to make your quest a little easier. The motifs here lend themselves quite well to oil painting.

The top two pictures are peaceful motifs, yet they are completely different. The tree-lined path provides an excellent opportunity to practice pointillism (see page 26). Don't lose yourself in the detail of the leaves; instead, concentrate on the overall effect of the light and the colors and shapes it produces.

The charm of the boat motif lies in the interplay of the different areas of the composition. Imagine using smooth gradations that contrast with lively, bold areas of color, and pay particular attention to the interplay of the different shapes.

Fresh flowers and a dried rose invite you to see how well you handle textures and the expressive elements of color. Try to incorporate the fresh flowers above into a simplified, abstract composition that doesn't lose the liveliness of the original.

The picture at the right offers an opportunity to create an interesting background that reflects the colors of the rose. The raw textures of the dried petals and leaves provide a contrast to the soft background.

60

The picture at the left could easily be made into an abstract painting. The shapes of the leaves form a pattern. You can put in the veins of the leaves with a palette knife, and the whole painting could be done in thick layers.

Below is a simple landscape. Notice the interplay of positive and negative space. The sky and the field could dissolve into one another. Try using unusual colors—who says parts of the field can't be violet?

Mixing colors with white is important for the still life above. A slightly overexposed photo such as this one can be an excellent motif for an oil painting. If you're looking for a photograph to paint from, it's a good idea not to use one that's perfect. The photo should simply be an inspiration and leave you the freedom to make changes and introduce exaggerations.

These boats in a canal in Venice (at left) can be approached in several ways. This motif is suitable for the use of a painting knife or precise brushwork. The contrast between the tranquil areas and the dynamic areas is especially interesting.

# Glossary

**aerial perspective**
The impression of distance produced by the atmosphere between an object and an observer. The greater the distance between object and observer, the more atmosphere there is between them. In painting, aerial perspective is represented by painting nearby objects in colors that are darker and more intense than the colors used to paint distant objects.

**cast shadow**
The shadow created when an opaque object blocks a light source. The size and shape of the cast shadow are influenced by the position of the light source.

**core shadow**
The shadow found on an object. The core shadow is always lighter than the cast shadow and gives an object its shape and three-dimensionality.

**cubism**
An artistic movement that developed in Paris in the early twentieth century. The founders, Picasso and Braque, were influenced by the ideas of Cézanne, who reduced natural forms to cubes, cylinders, and spheres. Although Cézanne used these geometric shapes to help build compositions, the cubists turned them into an art form. In cubist art, the motif is depicted in its basic shapes, sometimes leading to complete abstraction.

**dry-on-dry**
A technique of applying unthinned paint to a dry base. Depending on the texture of the surface, the artist can achieve interesting effects.

**glaze**
A thin, transparent layer of paint applied over dry paint. When applying glazes with oil paints, lean paint (low in oil content) should not be applied over fat paint (high in oil content); if it is, the result can be cracks in the surface of the painting.

**gradation**
A progression of tones, shades, or colors. A gradation can be a transition from dark to light or vice versa. In a gradation from dark to light, increasing amounts of white are mixed with the hue.

**impasto**
A thick application of paint. In oil painting, this technique involves the application of thick layers of unthinned or lightly thinned paint with a sturdy brush or palette knife so that the paint stands up from the surface, resulting in an obvious texture.

**intensity**
The strength of a color. Intensity denotes the degree to which a color is saturated with pigment.

**negative space**
The space between objects in a motif or between the motif and the frame.

**oil pastels**
A medium made from a mixture of pigment, wax, oil, and animal fat. The resulting paste is molded into sticks. Oil pastels are soluble in turpentine and are water resistant.

**plasticity**
The effect of three-dimensionality. Just as the sculptor can model a three-dimensional figure, the painter can use techniques to achieve the illusion of space.
*See also* **core shadow.**

**pointillism**
A Postimpressionist (late-nineteenth-century) technique characterized by the application of paint in numerous small dots. Seurat was the founder of pointillism; other well-known artists who used this technique include Picasso and Bignac.

**pop art**
A twentieth-century movement that represented banal objects as pieces of art. Pop art developed in the 1950s and 1960s as a reaction against abstract expressionism. The pop artists saw artistic value in even the smallest objects of everyday life. They also parodied contemporary "plastic" society.

**positive space**
The areas formed by objects in a painting. Positive and negative space is always interrelated.

**surrealism**
A movement in late-nineteenth- and early-twentieth-century art that used the psychology of Freud to try to express the workings of the subconscious. The surrealists believed that dreams, drugs, and hypnosis could open the door to the subconscious, which they viewed as the true reality. Surrealism found its way into the visual arts through the paintings of Giorgio de Chirico and Max Ernst. Other well-known surrealists include Picasso, Klee, Dali, Miró, and Magritte.

**tonal value**
The degree of darkness or lightness in a color, measured on a scale of gradations between black and white. Pure colors possess a value; for example, yellow is the lightest hue and violet is the darkest.

**wet-in-wet**
A technique of working with fresh paint on a wet surface. Working wet-in-wet allows the artist to achieve soft blends and delicate contours.

# Index

## Credits

## Copyright

### *Getting Started in Oils*
### Recommended Readings

Foster, Walter T. *Mixing Colors and Materials To Use*. How To Series. Tustin, California: Walter Foster Publishing. 1989. #HT56. ISBN: 1-56010-046-X.

Palluth, William. *Painting In Oils*. Artist's Library Series. Tustin, California: Walter Foster Publishing. 1984. #AL01. ISBN: 0-929261-01-1.

Powell, William F. *Color (And How To Use It)*. Artist's Library Series. Tustin, California: Walter Foster Publishing. 1984. #AL05. ISBN: 0-929261-05-4.

————. *Oil Painting Materials (And Their Uses)*. Artist's Library Series. Tustin, California: Walter Foster Publishing. 1990. #AL17. ISBN: 1-56010-056-7.

Send for a free Walter Foster catalog: Walter Foster Publishing, 430 West Sixth Street, Tustin, CA 92680-9990.

# Artist's Workshop Series

The books in the Artist's Workshop series are written and designed to provide beginning and even more experienced artists with basic techniques and tips on painting in watercolors and oils. Taken together, these books represent a handy home library to which art enthusiasts can refer for both instruction and inspiration again and again.

Bagnall/Hille
**Getting Started in Watercolors**
A fascinating introduction to painting in watercolors. Practicing professional artists give step-by-step instruction in the basic techniques. Included are watercolor paintings by such famous masters as Turner, Dürer, and Cézanne. **AW02.**

Bagnall/Hille
**Getting Started in Oils**
A fascinating introduction to painting in oils. Practicing professional artists give step-by-step instruction in the basic techniques. Included are oil paintings by such famous masters as Picasso, Rembrandt, and Van Gogh. **AW01.**

Bagnall/Hille
**Watercolors—Landscape**
Learn to paint distant mountains, sparkling rivers, deep forests, and rolling fields. The numerous examples provide guidance and inspiration. Included are landscapes in watercolor by such famous masters as Cotman, Nolde, and Middleton. **AW03.**

Bagnall/Hille
**Oils—Still Life**
Learn to paint everyday objects—fruit, bowls, chairs, and flowers in a vase—in striking and revealing ways. The numerous examples provide guidance and inspiration. Included are still lifes in oil by such famous masters as Van Eyck, Morandi, and Braque. **AW04.**

For more information and a free catalog, write to Walter Foster Publishing, 430 West Sixth Street, Tustin, CA 92680-9990.